How to Find a Book

by Amanda StJohn

illustrated by
Bob Ostrom

The Child's World®

Published by The Child's World®
1980 Lookout Drive • Mankato, MN 56003-1705
800-599-READ • www.childsworld.com

Acknowledgments
The Child's World®: Mary Berendes, Publishing Director
The Design Lab: Design and production
Red Line Editorial: Editorial direction

ISBN 9781614732501
LCCN 2012932862

Printed in the United States of America
Mankato, MN
November 2012
PA02156

About the Author

Amanda StJohn is an author and public librarian.
She's fascinated by singing frogs and animal tracks
and enjoys apricot tea and knitting.

About the Illustrator

Bob Ostrom is an award-winning children's
illustrator. His work has been featured in
more than two hundred children's books and
publications. When Bob is not illustrating children's
books you can usually find him in a classroom or
online teaching kids how to draw.

Stew Rabbit and his best friend Opal Owl loved to read. They had many favorite books at home. They read their favorite books aloud to each other. They read them quietly to themselves. They shared these books with their siblings. It was great fun.

Then, one day, Opal said to Stew, "It's time to find something new to read."

Stew wiggled his nose. "How do we find something new to read?"

"Go to the library?" guessed Opal.

"Yes!" Stew cheered. "Great idea."

Stew's father also liked the idea. Together, they went to the library.

At the library, Opal went straight to the books on Egyptian mummies. These books were **nonfiction**. Librarians give every nonfiction book a number. The number for mummy books starts with 393.

Beatrix Potter wrote Stew's favorite books. He loved to read about Peter Rabbit. These books were **fiction**. Librarians put fiction books in order by the last name of the **author**. The Peter Rabbit books lived at P-O-T in the fiction section. P-O-T stood for Beatrix Potter.

Stew and Opal gathered a whole stack of books. "All done!" they announced.

"Wait a minute," said Stew's father. "I thought you wanted something new. You've read these already."

Stew and Opal looked at their books choices.

"Carrot sticks!" Stew said. "We only picked our favorite books again, Opal."

"Well," said Opal, "how do we find new book choices?"

Opal and Stew looked at Stew's father. Stew's father nodded toward Miss Mantis.

Miss Mantis was the children's librarian. On Wednesdays she read story hour for the children.

"Miss Mantis?" whispered Stew. "Do you know any good books to read?"

Miss Mantis smiled. "I have my favorites. What do you like to read about?"

"Mummies," answered Opal. "But I've read all the mummy books."

"Egyptian mummies, bog mummies, or Incan mummies?" asked Miss Mantis.

Opal's eyes widened. "You mean Egyptian mummies aren't the only kind?"

"Let's shine some light on the subject," Miss Mantis replied. She, Opal, and Stew went to a computer to search the **catalog**.

"For books in our library, search here," directed Miss Mantis. "First, click the type of search you would like to do. You can search by author, **title**, or subject."

"Well," said Opal. "'Incan mummies' is definitely not an author. It might be a book title, but probably there are lots of books about Incan mummies." Opal used the mouse to click "subject."

Miss Mantis continued. "Now, type 'Incan mummies' in the search box. Then, click 'search.'"

Opal didn't know how to spell "Incan." She sounded out, "Ink-an." She typed it the best she could. She spelled "mummies" perfectly and clicked "search."

The catalog bleeped. A message read: "Did you mean: Incan mummies?"

"Yes," said Opal to the catalog.

"You have to click 'Incan mummies,'" Stew offered.

Presto! The catalog gave Opal search results on Incan mummies.

"Twenty books? Woo-hooot! " Opal sang.

"Slow down," said Stew. "Don't forget—our library shares books with many libraries. We have to make sure the book is here, at O'Hare Public Library."

"How?" asked Opal.

"We look at the **record**," said Stew. He clicked on a search result. The record showed plenty of information. It named the book's title and author. It gave a short summary about the book. "Ah, here's what we want . . ."

Below the word *Location*, this book's record said, "Badger Public Library, Fern Community Library, O'Hare Public Library."

"It's here!" squealed Opal.

"What's the call number?" Stew asked.

Opal knew that a call number was a group of letters and numbers. Like an address, it would tell her where the Incan books lived in the library. Just as the Egyptian mummy books lived at the 393s, Incan mummy books had to live somewhere, too.

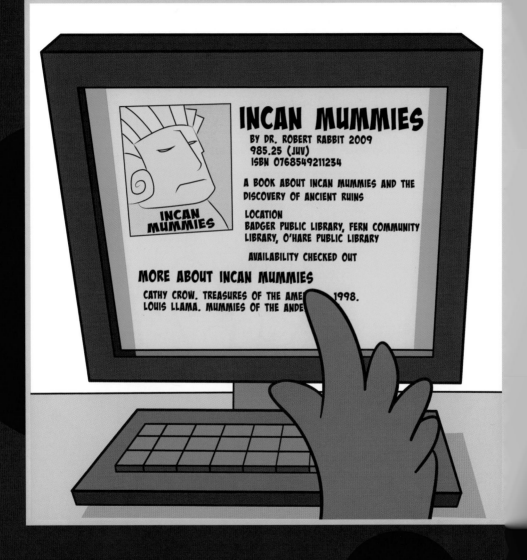

Opal looked for *Call Number* on the screen and said, "985.25."

Miss Mantis tapped Opal's shoulder. "Is this book suitable for children?"

Opal blushed. "Um . . ."

"Look for 'Juv.'" Stew helped. "Juvenile means kids."

Below *Call Number* Opal found 985.25 (Juv). "For kids! Now, let's go find it."

Opal and Stew searched the shelves for the book. They went to the nonfiction section. They started at the top shelf. They looked from left to right. When they didn't see 985, they moved down to the next shelf. They looked from left to right until they found 985.25. But the Incan mummy book was missing.

"Hey," whimpered Opal. "Why can't we find it?"

"Maybe we missed a detail in the record," answered Stew.

"Then," began Opal, "let's take a second look."

"Here!" Stew pointed to *Availability*. "This tells if the book is on the shelf or if it is checked out."

Beneath *Availability*, Opal read, "Checked out." Opal's shoulders sagged.

"It's all right," said Stew. "Let's look at more search results."

Opal brightened and clicked the back button. The computer went back to the list of search results. Together, she and Stew found a new Incan mummies book.

"Now," said Opal, "Let's do a checklist.

One: does O'Hare Library have a copy?"

"Check yes!" exclaimed Stew.

"Two: is this book for children?"

"Check yes!"

"Three: is this book on the shelf?"

"Check . . ." started Stew.

"Check yes!" Miss Mantis finished.

"Then," said Opal, "let's capture an Inca mummy."

Stew found the book.

"Woo-hoot!" Opal shook her tail feathers.

"Well done," said Miss Mantis to Stew. "You've saved the day."

"Like a superhero?" Stew didn't feel like a superhero. "It was a lot of work to find just one book."

"Tsk, tsk," said Miss Mantis. "You found a book—on your own. And it's a book that makes Opal happy."

"Yes," said Stew. "But if I walked around and pulled books off the shelf, I could find a stack of books in an instant."

Miss Mantis smiled. "Yes, you'd find plenty of books—farm books, origami books . . . but what does your heart want?"

"I just want cookbooks," beamed Stew. "I'm going to be a chef."

Miss Mantis squinted. "What do you know about becoming a chef?"

"I know plenty of recipes," answered Stew.

"Did you know chefs go to cooking schools?"

"Really?" Stew didn't know there were schools for cooks.

"And," added Miss Mantis, "there are pastry chefs, saucier chefs, sous chefs…"

Stew perked up. "Did you say soup chefs?"

"The sous chef is second in command," Miss Mantis smiled. "The saucier makes soupy sauces."

Stew didn't know why but his whiskers twitched. His heart tickled. "Sous chef," he whispered. "Saucier." Stew imagined he was wearing a tall, white chef's hat. He was stirring some alphabet soup.

"Miss Mantis?" Stew asked, "How do you spell sous chef?"

Soon, Stew and Opal were busy using the catalog. They looked for books about bog mummies. They looked for storybooks about rabbits and owls.

"Look for a book titled *I Want to Be a Chef*," offered Miss Mantis.

Stew's father helped, too. "Look for more books by the author of Opal's Incan mummy book."

At last, they had a stack of books that they'd never read before.

Stew's father was impressed with Opal and Stew's fine work. "What did you learn about using the catalog?" he asked.

"Well," joked Stew, "you just never know what great results will *turnip*!"

Glossary

author (AW-thur): The author is the writer of the story or book. Stew read several books by the same author.

catalog (KAT-uh-lawg): The catalog is the complete list of items a library has to offer. Stew and Opal searched the catalog for books to read.

fiction (FIK-shun): Fiction stories are stories about characters and events that are not real. Stew liked fiction books about rabbits.

nonfiction (NON-fik-shun): Nonfiction writings tell real facts about the world. Opal liked nonfiction books about mummies.

record (REK-urd): The record lists all the known details about a particular book, DVD, or other item in the library. Opal read the record to see if the book was in the library.

title (TYE-tul): The title is the name of the book. The title of Opal's book was *Mummies*.

Tips to Remember!

- Use the catalog to find books you've never read before.

- If the book you want is missing on the shelf, the catalog can tell you why. It might be checked out to someone else.

- Make sure the book you want says "J" or "JUV"—that means for kids.

- Ask your children's librarian which books he or she loves to read.

Web Sites

Visit our Web site for links about library skills: childsworld.com/links

Note to Parents, Teachers, and Librarians: We routinely verify our Web links to make sure they are safe and active sites. So encourage your readers to check them out!

Books

Bennett, Elizabeth. *A Book for Chester*. New York: Scholastic, 2011.

Buzzeo, Toni. *The Great Dewey Hunt*. Janesville, WI: Upstart Books: 2009.

Hynson, Colin. *You Wouldn't Want to Be an Inca Mummy!: A One-Way Journey You'd Rather Not Make*. New York: Franklin Watts, 2008.

Liebman, Dan. *I Want to Be a Chef*. Richmond Hill, ONT: Firefly Books, 2012.